Y0-BZY-326

annie sloan's
PAINTED GARDEN

annie sloan's
PAINTED GARDEN

25 easy outdoor paint effects to transform any surface

Annie Sloan

CICO BOOKS

London

First published in 2003 by Cico Books Ltd
32 Great Sutton Street London EC1V 0NB

Copyright © Cico Books 2003

The right of Annie Sloan to be identified as author of this
text has been asserted by her in accordance with the
Copyright, Designs and Patents Act of 1988.

All rights reserved. No part of this publication may be
reproduced, stored in or introduced into a retrieval system,
or transmitted in any form or by any means, electronic,
mechanical, photocopying, recording or otherwise, without
the prior written permission of the copyright holder and
publisher.

10 9 8 7 6 5 4 3 2 1

A CIP catalogue record for this book is available from the
British Library

ISBN 1 903116 62 7

Editor: Ian Kearey
Designer: Jon Raimes
Photographer: Tino Tedaldi

Printed and bound in China

contents

introduction: the painted garden

Stepping out into the garden with your paintbrush is a great adventure. I first became aware of the extraordinary power of color in a garden when a friend, faced with a garden with a plain picket fence and simple plants, dramatically improved it when she painted the fence a beautiful powdery blue. As we noticed all sorts of different-colored and shaped leaves and plants growing up against a contrasting color, the garden seemed to spring into existence. So, paint that old wooden bench, your unused table, or an old garden ornament, and you will be able to see how an afternoon spent painting brings your garden to life with minimum effort. To me, now, a garden without a painted wall, decorated pots, or colorful chairs and tables seems unfinished.

Choosing the colors of your garden-decorating scheme is both fun and a challenge. For expert tips on how to match your own favorite shades of the rainbow with the subtleties of plant colors from pale gray-green to the hot tones of summer flowers, consult the range of gardens worldwide that I have showcased in chapter 2, "Color in the Garden." As with every successful home-design scheme, working out how to really make the most of your space is key. In chapter 3, "Areas and Features of the Garden," I have shown how to work your yard or garden to make a truly comprehensive living space , from creating a charming dining space for the entire family to the placing of pots and planters for the most dramatic effect.

With easy-to-use water-based paints in a rainbow of tones and shades, modern paint effects and finishes, and the wonderful new metallic and distressed-effect paints now on the market, your outdoor space can now be more than just flowers and foliage. The 25 easy projects in this book show you how to transform your garden into the most stylish space in the home. Our garden centers and home improvement stores today are filled with all sorts of useful and inexpensive products that can be given a unique and beautiful finish. Although plastic might be a popular bargain buy, light to carry, weatherproof, and practical, it does not initially look appealing or stylish. However, now you can add colors and create paint effects so cheaply and easily, even the most humble planter becomes a true style statement. Try this with garden furniture; even a worn, used set of plastic tables and chairs can be given a new lease on life. Also, very reasonably priced, modern garden ornaments can be a very inspiring source for a stunning centerpiece; spheres of different sizes, pyramids, and a host of statue styles from every culture are now available in molded resins and cement mixes. Once you have chosen the scale of your piece, from kitsch to grand and classically European, give your bargain buy the look of a much-loved heirloom with a simple paint effect.

Fabric, wood, and metal can be revitalized through paint, too, so look in your garden shed and see what you can find to resurrect and recycle. And don't forget to paint the garden shed! For a finishing touch, remember that paint is not the only way to bring color and light to your garden—I have included mosaic projects that make the most of the subtle, weather-worn colors of pebbles and stones for an understated, natural outdoor style. Whether your garden is traditional, grand, modern, or just a tiny paved yard, my *Painted Garden* will show you how to bring color and style to outdoor living.

materials and paints

Decorating your garden using paints and other materials presents few problems even to the beginner—but no matter how simple the project, it is always a good idea to familiarize yourself with the key materials you need. Using the many new paints on the market, plastics and metals can now become the basis for a paint transformation, as can used or worn items, in addition to the more traditional materials, such as stone and terra-cotta. The wide range of hard-wearing paints now available that are suitable for the garden includes textured, metallic, and flat paints.

As you start to decorate, remember that color in the garden can be achieved by more than paint—discover the variety of materials available for making mosaics, from classic pebble patterns to innovative modern gravels and colored grouts. For a finishing touch, learn how to choose brushes and use varnishes and sealers on your finished pieces for extra durability.

surfaces, brushes, and preparation

Today terra-cotta, cement, wood, metal, plastic, and even fabrics can be painted and completely transformed into something modern and exciting. The projects in this book are suitable for a wide variety of garden materials, including objects you wish to recycle, pots and planters that need a new lease on life, faded existing features, and inexpensive new buys that need an individual touch.

surfaces

Plastic makes up a vast variety of plant containers and garden furniture. It is useful for large pots, because a large stone or pottery container will be very heavy to move around the garden, particularly when filled with soil and plants.

Metals can also be painted. Existing features or ornaments may need treating with a sealer to prevent rust. But why not make the most of the rusting quality of metals, either by creating your own rust finish (see page 78), or by using recycled metals? Galvanized iron and aluminum are nonrusting, and therefore are great materials.

Cement and *plaster* ornaments come in a choice of figures, animals, and sculptures, as well as birds, angels, and more abstract modern shapes. These pieces take paint and paint effects well.

Terra-cotta is always popular in the garden. A porous material, it takes paint beautifully, because the paint is absorbed through the surface rather than sitting on top as a coating.

Wood is ideal for decorating, and as an alternative to painting. Large wooden pieces or features can be stained to allow the natural pattern of the grain to show through.

Stones and *pebbles* are a delight in any garden, either left in their natural, gentle shades or painted for incidental touches of color around the base of a tree, in a fountain, or as part of a border.

Fabrics can be painted for the garden with waterproof fabric paint. This is the perfect way to revive old garden umbrellas, chairs, and awnings, which often fade in sunlight.

Ceramics can be painted, although shiny surfaces may need to be sealed so paint can adhere.

brushes

When choosing a brush, look to buy standard decorating brushes—there are no special brushes for outdoor work. Most paintbrushes range from 12mm to 100mm. In general, use two brushes— a larger one, about 50–75mm, to cover the main body of the project, and a finer brush, 12–38mm, for the intricate finishing process.

Use your paintbrush in the same way as for interior work—when you apply the paint, do not overload the brush or apply too much paint in one stroke. To prevent brush marks from showing, use straight, sweeping strokes.

To load a brush correctly, immerse a third or a half of the brush into the paint can, then press the brush against the side of the can to remove excess paint. As you apply paint, cover the surface well, then use the tip of the brush to sweep lightly over the almost-finished surface, spreading the paint out over the area and thinning the coating. Always apply a second coat if the first one looks too thin.

preparation

PRIMING

Priming is applying the preliminary coat to a surface before applying paint. Some surfaces, such as very shiny plastic, or ceramics, need to be primed with a proprietary product that will allow paint to adhere to them. It is also a good idea to prime a metal that can rust with metal primer, usually red oxide metal paint.

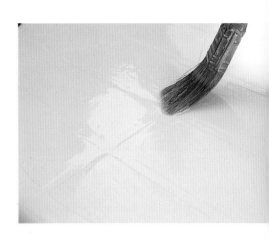

SEALING

Before painting, you will need to seal porous surfaces such as terra-cotta so paint will adhere (*left*). When you finish your work, you will also need to seal the piece for protection. Most metallic paints should be sealed, and patina finishes will benefit, particularly if they come into contact with skin. Chalk paints and lime wash do not need to be sealed.

PREPARING METAL FOR PAINTING

1 To remove flaking paint and to even the surface, sand over with coarse-grade abrasive paper and dust off.

2 Any areas of rust on the metal parts must be treated. Following the manufacturer's instructions, paint one or more coats of rust inhibitor over all signs of rust, however faint, and allow to dry.

colored paints

There are more paints on the market today that can be used in the garden than ever before. The paints are either water-based, which tend to have a matte finish, or oil-based, which give a shinier finish. To create the colors throughout this book, I have used water-based paints, except where I have made a paint for a specific purpose (as for the green tree house on page 116), or have used a stain (as for the tablecloth effect on page 94)—both of these materials are oil-based.

HOT COLORS

Hot colors are all those connected with fire—red, orange, and yellow. Purple is included here, but it is on the borderline and could be included in cool colors, depending on how much blue there is in it. In the garden— where it is next to green foliage, it is generally a warm color.

The flat paints used for the projects are called *chalk paints* because of their high chalk-type content. This makes a very matte surface that hardens over time, so chalk paints last well in all types of weathers. One advantage over other water-based paints is that they can be used over almost any surface, from plastic to metal, as long as the surface is clean and free of grease. Their matte quality gives painted items a mellow, soft look. The surface painted by oil-based paints tends to be hard and often shiny, a finish contrary to the natural feel of a garden. Chalk paints also cover very well because of their high pigmentation and creamy texture.

Lime wash is a traditional paint, dating back centuries, that is available from specialty suppliers. In some ways, it behaves like a stain, because it is absorbed into the surface, but it gives the thick coverage of a paint. Lime wash can be used on brick or wood, and has a soft, full effect.

Pigments are a very satisfying way of adding color to a whole host of materials, from paints to varnish to cement. Adding pigment can change the color of an existing paint, tint a stain, or color "uncolored" or white products.

COOL COLORS

All the different blues and greens are cool, especially in the garden, where there is a lot of green foliage. For maximum impact, use coolest shades for paints and plants so that any flowers, particularly those in warm colors, really stand out.

distressed and metallic paints

One of the great new innovations of recent years has been the introduction of paints that create metallic effects. The paints used throughout this book are designed to be used outdoors, and contain real ground metal, which gives the best result of all for solid, metallic looks.

With all of these products, it is vital to read and follow the manufacturers' instructions—and this includes the preparation that must be done before you begin to use the product. Modern technology allows us to make wonderful effects—but only if we use them in the way they were intended to be employed!

copper and bronze

copper

Paint on copper in smooth strokes with a brush, or stipple on with a brush or sponge to give a textured or hammered look. Copper takes patination very well, either covering the whole surface or leaving some areas free (see page 19). Copper needs to be sealed to stop it from tarnishing, especially in a garden.

choosing metallic paint

The choice of metals used is broad enough for you to experiment with different finishes. Silver paint, for example, can simulate aluminum, and you can mix two metallic paints together to get the color you want—I often mix a little steel paint into silver to get a more muted silver for an antique effect.

Metallic paints should always be sealed because they tarnish (see page 11), particularly in a damp outdoor atmosphere.

bronze

Bronze is traditionally a mix of copper and tin, but can contain other metals, such as manganese or aluminum. The color varies from quite golden to copper. It patinates (see page 19) by blackening, leaving areas of golden or copper color.

silver, steel, and gold

how to use metallic paint

Metallic colors can be painted on any surface. An old, rusty metal can be changed into a new metal, such as shiny silver, and a new piece of wood can be transformed while remaining perfectly sturdy. Metallic paints are simple to use, although certain surfaces may need preparation (see page 11), and a rusty surface will need to be sanded to remove old rust, and then sealed with a proprietary rust sealer. To paint cloth such as canvas, seal the surface to stop the paint from sinking in, and seal other very absorbent surfaces, such as plaster, terra-cotta, and wood , to make the paint go further—sealer is less expensive than paint.

silver and steel

Various silver colors are available in metallic paints, from platinum to warm silver, as well as steel. These can be mixed to make a particular color. Most of these colors do not react with patinating fluid (see page 19), but some products react to make a silver-copper look. These paints can be applied with a rag or sponge. Use a brush to imitate shiny silver, making the brush strokes look like brushed metal.

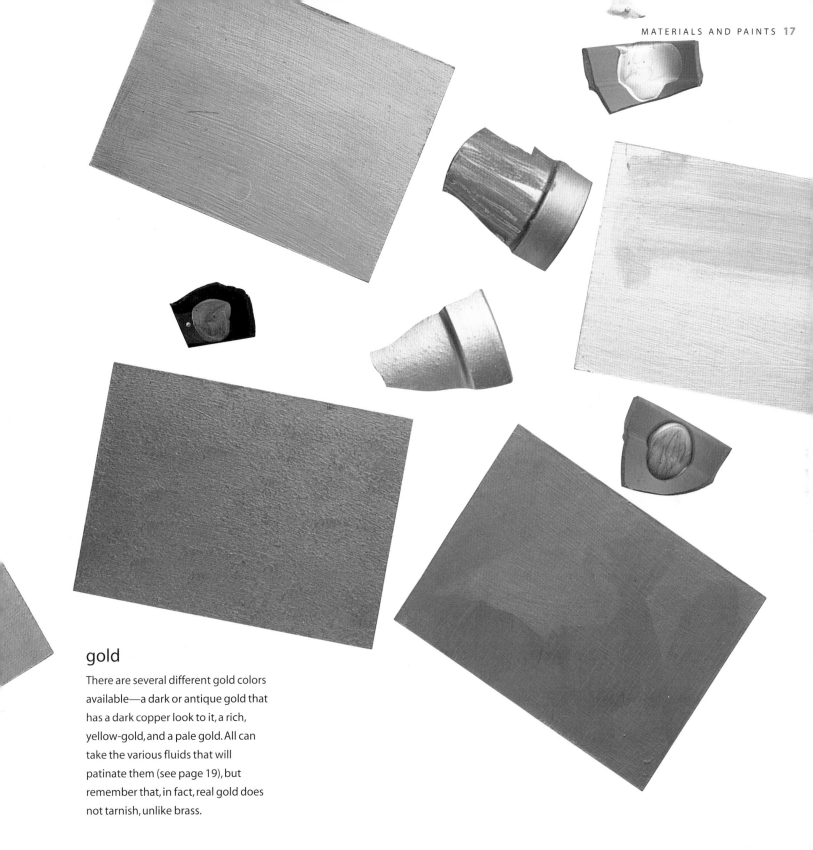

gold

There are several different gold colors available—a dark or antique gold that has a dark copper look to it, a rich, yellow-gold, and a pale gold. All can take the various fluids that will patinate them (see page 19), but remember that, in fact, real gold does not tarnish, unlike brass.

metallic blue, pewter, and patinas

metallic blue and pewter

Colored metallic finishes can be applied with a brush or a sponge. The finish has a shimmering look to it—it cannot be patinated, and is best left looking new and shiny. Pewter is a very deep, warm gray, and gives a deep, dull finish. It is applied using a stippling technique. The same color can be used to imitate lead.

patinas

Metals that are not new, even if kept polished, have a varied color to them with lots of depth, known as the patina (*above right*). This effect can be achieved using the blue and green patination liquids available for use on metal paints (*above*). Rust (*right*) is a form of patination and is applied to still-wet or damp metal paint. Patinating fluids are applied using a brush, wiping some areas with a rag, or working with a spray gun. The wetter the paint, the stronger the color will be. If there is a heavy layer of paint on a nonabsorbing surface, the patina finish you add will produce a very bright effect shown (*below right*). Sealing patinated pieces will prevent further tarnish and oxidization; you may choose not to seal a rust finish. As with all paint effects, it is vital to follow the manufacturers' instructions for a good finish—it is worth checking on a website if you are not sure about which finish to use.

paint effects

When you're choosing a paint to enhance pots and other ornaments and surfaces in the garden, remember that you do not need to stick to matte paint. Textured effects offer depth and interest, although in the garden you should be careful not to overwhelm the liveliness of your plants. Keep colors subtle— in a garden, any effect will look stronger and provide a strong contrast. Paler colors and pastels tend to produce a more elegant and sophisticated look, while warm, earthy colors produce a country-style finish.

One of the delights of an old, established garden is the way in which the paint has aged and blistered off surfaces, leaving areas of another color. You can create this fashionably aged look with the crackle-glaze technique, seen in the garden shed project on page 90, and also achieve the two-colored look while at the same time maintaining the strength and protective qualities of the paint.

There are many traditionally designed pots and statues in garden centers, molded from both stone and plastic. For a stunning, yet inexpensive transformation, try creating a marble effect to match a traditional container, which you can buy as a concrete copy of an original (see page 104). If the surface is rough, a stone effect also suits well (see page 92), but stamped or molded containers will benefit from a wiped effect, where the top layer of paint is removed to improve definition on the underlying pattern. If your feature or area is too smooth and uninteresting, try adding sand to the paint to create strong texture (see page 120).

Creating patterned features in the garden using stamping and stencils is another option. Start by experimenting with designs on a piece of paper, remembering to keep the design graphic and simple, whether you prefer abstract shapes or more traditional motifs. The regular stamping on the fence (see page 118) turns a simple pattern into rows, or "streets," of little houses— alternatively, you could simply stamp rectangles and squares to create a random backdrop on a shed, or to create a mural.

mosaic materials

When most of us first think about using mosaics, we imagine patterns consisting of small, square tiles set into cement—in the style of ancient Greek or Roman mosaics—but this is too narrow a definition for the wide variety of materials and cements that can be used in the garden. To make a mosaic, anything that can be stuck onto a piece of cement, and that will withstand the weather, can be used. Try finding recycled, broken, or old objects that can be given new life as mosaic work—in terms of "secondhand" materials, I have so far found and used plates, buttons, gravel, mirrors, old tiles, and pieces of marble in my mosaics. If you are lucky enough to find small fossils, use them as a centerpiece for a charming, unique mosaic, either on their own or in combination with more common source materials. Once you have made your selection, practice arranging the pattern on a piece of paper until you are satisfied with the size, shape, and design, and trim the mosaic pieces if necessary to make sure they fit snugly together.

For more traditional glass or metallic mosaic pieces, there is a variety of choices— a good supplier will offer a selection of ready-made mosaic tiles in everything from a rainbow of matte, natural colors to pearled glass and tiny, mirrored pieces.

Getting started with mosaic does not require too many specialized pieces of equipment, but a few essential items will allow you to work more quickly and safely. If you are going to make mosaic pieces from ceramics such as tiles or plates, a tile cutter will allow you to tailor the shape and size of your pieces. If you are using tile cutters or nippers, always wear a pair of tough gloves while holding sharp ceramic pieces to trim, and do not start work without wearing safety glasses or goggles to protect your eyes from flying shards.

The finished effect of a mosaic has as much to do with the surrounding of the pieces, and the pattern of the glue or grout, as with the pieces themselves. Once you are happy with your finished design on paper, you might need to trim the mosaic pieces to make sure they fit snugly together. Many beginners prefer to use white wood glue to stick the pieces down, but as you develop your skills, you may prefer to use mosaic cement, which allows you to embed the pieces more easily— this is available from good craft stores or specialty mosaic suppliers.

For a smooth, professional-looking finish, use one of the many grouts on the market. In the garden, always use a waterproof grout, often sold as swimming-pool grout, available from home stores and garden centers. Most are white and off-white, but using colored grouts opens up all sorts of creative possibilities. You can also color a pale grout yourself by mixing in pigment available from craft stores.

For floors, there are all sorts of wonderful natural materials to be found at garden centers—pebbles of almost every hue can be purchased, including white, black, ocher, blue, red, yellow, and mauve, as well as green and gray slate pieces. In addition, all kinds of different-colored gravels, designed for the bottom of fish tanks, are available from pet stores. For a durable floor mosaic, always use stone pieces that are at least 2 in. across; they will hold more firmly in the cement.

color in the garden

How do you choose the colors to use in your garden so it looks harmonious and not a jumbled mess? First, you have to decide what kind of garden you want. If you want colors to help bring out the colors of the flowers, then the paint has to take a backseat and not dominate—pale, dark, or muted colors will do the job. If you want the colors to be in the architecture and furniture, then you will probably need brighter colors.

Which particular hue you choose has to do with the colors of the flowers and the foliage. If you are a plant person first and foremost, you will probably want to have colors that bring out the colors of your plants. By considering the colors of the leaves alone, a huge range of greens is introduced, from lime green and greens we usually call leaf greens to the silver-grays and dark forest greens. Besides greens, there is also copper-red and black foliage, and some grasses are sand-colored.

multicolors

Creating a multicolor theme is not just a matter of letting it develop naturally. You have to keep an eye on it, otherwise it will end up with all sorts of colors and look messy. If you choose the bright route, one color should be the main one so other colors can react to it.

Left: Bold, wild flowers need strongly colored pots—bright green, Hawaiian pink, and strong yellow.

Below: A simple, wooden picket fence is painted to resemble colored pencils.

Above: In the corner of a garden, dappled light through the trees falls on these pearly button boxes, which catch the light so they shine.

Below: A garden of harlequin colors and patterns in Arizona has ceramic wall plaques on an orange wall.

Left: Half practical and half ornamental, this delightful home-made chair was painted and stained in a simple color combination.

Left: Ice-cream colors for a hot summer's day—these simple garden chairs were painted in pastel stripes using sample cans of paint.

Below: For a mainly foliage garden, strongly colored walls and planters are the theme. Here, the lower green and blue planters are a steadying influence for the clashing, shocking pink with a scarlet red wall behind it.

green and white

White is very classical, romantic, and nostalgic—but unless you use it in a definite and deliberate way, it can be overlooked. You can make a huge impact by using white flowers and silver foliage, and carrying the idea into all areas of the garden with paint, pebbles, shells, and marble. Off-white gives a traditional look, and bright white a contemporary look.

Above: White woodwork needs to work for you, so add more white in the garden. This mosaic pot has little daisies designed on a gray background, making a simple and fresh addition to the white daisies planted in it.

Above right: Concrete animals can look a little kitsch, but when painted in white they take on a clean, abstract look. Placed in a flowerbed, this duck's head pokes up through foliage, looking both charming and a little comical.

Left: Bleached white decking with primary blue and yellow has a fresh, bright, clean look.

Right: In shadow, white looks gray, so the two colors work well together, complementing each other in a neutral way.

Left: Classical ruins lie in a garden under the trees. This head, made from a cement-based product, has been painted off-white, and was given the look of old marble by rubbing dark brown and black in the recesses.

green, black, and gray

Black and gray are not obvious colors to use in the garden, but they can have a marvelous effect, particularly as a backdrop for brightly colored flowers and foliage—especially in full sunlight. Bright, light colors look very dramatic and show up well against such a background.

Left: A black-stained garden bench makes a great silhouette against the grass.

Below left: A gray lion made of resin, guarding the entrance to a country house, lies under a dark green yew tree.

Below: Black trellis makes an unobtrusive but elegant divider.

Right: The painted brick wall gives the silver-gray zinc and wire containers a sympathetic partner. The interest is in the sculptural quality, as well as the simple colors.

Above: A warm, ocher-painted wall is perfect in this courtyard garden, with the natural colors in the brick floor and wooden chair evoking an exotic corner of North Africa.

Right: Paint a plastic pot with iron paint and rust solution, leaving it to darken. The softness of the gray-green of the succulent and lavender plant go well with the sharper yellow-orange.

green, yellow, and orange

Yellow has two very distinct, polarized personalities. The first, characterized by bright lemon shades, is crisp, cool, and fresh, while the other, demonstrated by mellow ochers, is warm and soft. Gold looks yellow, too, as it glints in the sunshine.

Below: A tarnished copper Moroccan lantern with a hint of turquoise verdigris picks up on the earthy brown in both the natural wood and the ocher wood.

Right: This wooden window box was painted in yellow ocher and dabbed with a small, square sponge in a dark red oxide, to create a painted texture.

Above: Looking like it is in the south of France or Tuscany, a grapevine works its way along a trellis against a muted yellow wall in a sheltered garden. This yellow needs a strong green to really make an impact.

green and yellow

Above: Carved from rusted iron, this playful mermaid provides a pleasant diversion in a bed of wild flowers.

Above right: Strong yellow makes a terrific, warm glow at night and helps reflect light. If you have a garden that you will be using a lot at night, this is a good choice.

Far right: Yellow, gray, and a little blue work well together. The yellow-painted wall is used to cheer up rather austere gray and silver architectural features, and gives a hint of the exotic to match the strong foliage.

Right: The yellow-painted bench makes a delightfully colorful statement and enhances the mosaic patchwork wall behind.

green and blue

Everything in the garden works with blue. This color stands out since there are few blue flowers to fight for its attention. It also makes a good background partner with green foliage, since green and blue are both cool colors.

Left: The cobalt blue of this plastic pot enhances the hot colors of summer geraniums. I scratched a pattern into the wet paint, to reveal the orange of the pot beneath it.

Above left: A fence painted with a soft, warm blue with a hint of mauve, sets the scene for a sky-colored backdrop for the greenery.

Below left: You don't have to use a lot of blue to make an impact in the garden— sometimes one small feature can work well.

Above: The garden shed has been painted a positive blue and made inviting with a trellis and flowers around the door. The yellow-green leaves stand out against the blue.

Above: The vivid blue gives the wall real solidity in contrast to the greenery above. The warm reds of the cushions, flowers, and decorations help to create a feeling of coziness.

Right: This big plastic pot was painted warm blue for a Moroccan-style garden. Forest-green leaves and a scarlet iris bring all the primary colors together for maximum impact.

Above: (left) The metallic, blue-painted ball by the water reflects the light and makes an unusual partner with the classic urn on its blue base; (center) the old blue bench has gradually peeled and worn away, resulting in a delightfully nostalgic look; (right) a large pot decorated with broken plates and grouted in blue looks great against the brick wall and floor.

Left: Not all leaves are green. The blue-painted fence is a perfect way to show off beautiful copper-red leaves.

Right: Blue and white always work well together, and the greenery trailing over the trellis frame is understated.

Right: A dark blue bench against a red brick wall in a sunless part of the garden with few plants looks colorful and interesting.

Top: Honeysuckle trails around this wrought-iron fence now rusting gently. Re-create this with paint and rust-maker to give texture and color.

Above: A blue planter overspilling with unlikely black plants makes a dramatic pool of color, the edges tinted with gleaming copper.

Left: This home-made obelisk painted in blue gives height and color for the flowers to work against.

green and green

Traditional forest and grass greens merge into the background, but more elegant and unusual are soft, sage greens and olive greens, similar to silvery green foliage, that look wonderful on doors and pots. Yellowed lime colors and fresh new greens are quite radical and look great with dark foliage and bright flowers.

Left: This table and planter, painted in a complex gray-green color, match the many variations of greens in the moss and plants around them.

Left: On this trellis, I made the dark green a little brighter than usual so it is more apparent. Pink and red are the complementary colors of green, so this will give the flowers the maximum contrast.

Left: This striped pot works well with foliage plants, because it helps to balance the plainness of the plants. I printed a design on the pot using greens and terracotta colors that always bring out a plant.

Below: This great home-made bench, made from old pallets, has been painted a faded aqua, and the seat covers have been chosen to match.

Right: Nasturtiums spill over in lavish cascades. The color of the leaves is light and yellowish, and the flowers are bold and vivid. Here, they are in a deep-green-painted container.

Below: An old trellis with peeling and flaking aqua paint, trailing with ivy, has an old Victorian look of summers past.

green, red, purple, and pink

Red makes a huge impression in any garden, particularly if you use bright red. Purple can be painted on pots, fences, and pergolas for plants to climb over. Pale pink has a sweet and relaxing effect, while bright pink acts like red, shouting for attention. Pastel pinks are reminiscent of terra-cotta pinks.

Above: This pot of chives has little purple blooms. The crumbly lichen texture on the main part of the pot looked messy, so I cleaned it up by painting the rim and the edge of the saucer of the pot in the same purple.

Right: Bright red is an incredibly bold color to paint on a wall—this was used in an exhibition where an audacious statement was needed to set off the shell shape and the foliage.

Above right: An excellent and unusual combination of colors painted on a variation of the picket fence—smoky pink with candy pink and a spot of Parma violet—is pleasingly old-fashioned.

Above left: This mosaic angel hangs modestly on the wall, patiently holding a little pot in which a plant grows. Her red dress, golden wings, and orange hair are made of broken tiles.

Right: This red bench cheers me up in the winter as a bright, colorful spot in a bare garden. Painted several years ago with a mixture of boiled linseed oil and Chinese scarlet pigment, it has survived exposure to the elements extremely well.

Left: The color of terra-cotta pots can vary from orange to dusky pink. Choose the pink tones and paint the others pink.

Right: This gently bubbling fountain has been given extra interest by pink- and blue-painted pebbles being placed around it.

Left: The house is painted in a warm, rich cherry red, edged with soldier blue and smoky pink. The painted pot and the pink sculpture echo the colors of the house and jump with vitality.

Right: This chair has been painted in brilliant pink and yellow. The effect can be achieved easily by using two cans of spray paint and making trails and patches of the colors.

Left: I painted this bamboo wigwam with plum-color paint, and set it in the garden bed, both as an ornament to give height to the bed, and as a support for the climbing roses.

Above: This old bamboo planter had seen better days but was a good shape. I painted it gray-lilac, and filled it with a mixture of colors that allows green foliage and flowers to come to the front.

green, naturals, and terra-cotta

Terra-cotta is the main color of pots in most gardens, but consider it as a color for walls. It is a natural mate for nearly everything— though yellows don't always look their best with it, especially if the terra-cotta is a little pink. Chocolate brown, the color of dark wood, is the strong, silent type, pushing bright oranges and purples into the foreground. Using the colors of pebbles, stones, gravel, sand, and slate provides a natural focus.

Left: Some brown and earth-red pigments turn into mellow pinks when white is added. A reddish earth color was applied to this bench so it fits in with the terra-cotta pots.

Right: On this very rough old wall, a pink-tinged lime wash gives a homey backdrop for the plants. The old turquoise-green door helps bring it to life.

Above: Lime-washed walls colored with earthy ocher-red give a feeling of softness and space.

Right: This wall's rich, warm color has a very smooth and slightly shiny finish called polished plaster, achieved by using a special mix including marble dust.

Left: Just one different stepping stone among paving slabs, this is made of cement decorated with a simple mosaic of a butterfly in natural browns.

Right: Terra-cotta pots and bricks are the mainstays of gardens all over the world. The combination of purple plants and green looks stunning.

Far left: Resting on the gravel by the edge of a flowerbed, this mosaic ball, incorporating real fossils as well as fossil and shell designs, makes a subtle and unobtrusive ornament.

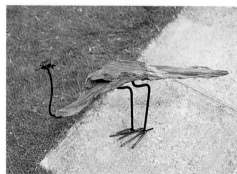

Left: This wooden picket fence was stained with an environmental herb and resin oil that incorporated a pink pigment.

Above: Many people like to use the color, feel, and texture of driftwood. With added legs and head, this piece turns into a bird on the path.

green and metallics

Luxurious gold, shiny copper, and polished bronze glint in the sunshine and are great additions to any open space. With modern paints we now can have these colors in the garden, adding a light-reflective element to the space. Like water and mirrors, metallics glint at different times of the day, so they add a bit of drama to the garden.

Above: The soft blue-green of the succulents is enhanced by introducing a copper-painted pebble into a copper-painted terra-cotta bowl.

Top: Pieces of scrap metal marked by rust and tarnishing have been made into a delightful, ornamental, inquisitive bird by a rosemary bush.

Above: Metallic colors don't have to be confined to ornaments or furniture in the garden—as is demonstrated by this aluminum-colored floor.

Above: A plastic insect, found in a garden supply center, was decorated in bright colors, but, painted in metallics, it took on a more interesting look.

Right: Old chairs painted with silver and metallic blue, united with a new table, look stunning in the summer evening light.

areas and features
of the garden

As we bring the house more and more out into the garden, we need to look at a wider range of different themes and styles. In the following pages you will find a number of different solutions on how to tackle these areas.

So many different decorative elements are possible in a garden. Most gardens do not possess all the areas shown here, but you will certainly have a few of them, such as a wall or fence, a sitting or dining area, or a path. Not every garden is lucky enough to have a guest house, but if you have a garden shed, you could pretend and turn it into a romantic hideaway. Whatever size your garden, you can have pots and planters in some shape or form, and maybe an ornament or two.

the dining area

The dining area is probably the most important part of the garden, because this is where we sit, relax, and admire our surroundings. This area may be small, private, and informal—ideal for a quiet drink in the evening—or it may be organized for entertaining family and friends for meals. Whatever function it serves, there is a variety of different ways to give it focus or intimacy.

Right: Wood, brick, and canvas are the natural materials used here. The fencing is used as a back rest for the seating area.

Right: You need a big garden to achieve this effect. The symmetry of the garden gives a wonderful focus to the table and chairs, situated on a round mosaic of bricks.

Left: Feeling a little like a tree house, placed as it is above the garden, this dining area fits comfortably into the background with brown woodwork and green fabrics. The purple chairs give a boost of color.

Above: If you have the space, why not combine a pond with the dining area? The irregularly shaped stepping stones across the water lend a rustic charm to this scene and set the quiet, muted tones.

Left: A modern courtyard garden has a blue-painted wall behind a simple semicircular pool, giving a feeling of enclosure and depth at the same time.

Above: Paint furniture with metallic paint, both for strength and a modern look that gives a new dimension to the garden with its reflective shine.

Right: Surrounded by white, green, and terra-cotta walls, trellis, and pots, the blue-painted table and chairs are the center of attention in this little enclosed garden.

Right: An old plastic table has been reinvented to look like a heavy, bronze one, but is still as light as a feather.

Right: These beautiful earth and ocher walls are varied in color to give a lime-washed effect, creating a soft, warm, and glowing backdrop for plants. The off-white stone of the Italianate fountain, window, and planter helps to set off the yellow.

the patio garden

The patio or courtyard garden is usually small and relies on a lot of architectural features, with plants being grown in pots. This is often an intimate space surrounded by walls, and you have to work on the decoration to make it feel and look attractive, rather than like a scrappy backyard. Colored walls and decorative pots are good ways to start.

Above: This uses similar colors to the garden opposite, but in a more contemporary setting. The soft ocher-brown of the wooden wall contrasts well with the cleaner gray-white of the stone pavers, pebbles, and painted wall.

Left: This inventive garden makes the most of a small area. The rich blue on the wall gives a feeling of depth, like an endless sky, and the mirror in the "window" increases the illusion of space. The small pool, decorated in blue and white mosaic, gives off a reflection, and the pebble designs on the floor are another strong feature.

Right: Even in this enclosed patio garden, the light colors of the striped fabric, off-white benches, and pale pebbles create a bright, airy feeling.

Left: The garden can be a refuge, with secret places that only you know about. Hidden among the foliage of the patio part of this garden are small, personal items, such as a small Buddha, a shell plaque, and other miniature sculptures.

Far right: Any patio or courtyard needs interesting pots, either filled with plants or empty. The middle large pot is painted gold, adding a subtle glow to the natural colors of its neighbors.

ornaments

There are few gardens that do not contain something that is purely ornamental. Plants give a garden height and focus, but there is something very refreshing about an inanimate object in their midst. This object can be placed in a flowerbed, at the end of a path, or on a wall, or can even nestle half-hidden among plants to be discovered with surprise.

Above left: You can make a simple and inexpensive ornament by sticking shells into a cement surface—or perhaps use old keys, coins, or even small garden tools.

Left: A modern sculptural piece of decoration gives style to a garden. These days, garden centers sell all sorts of ornaments, giving you a wide choice.

Above: A painted, cement-molded cherub, the classic form of ornamentation, can look classy, so long as it is the right scale for the garden in which it stands.

Right: An oriental theme, here a verdigris Buddha, can be pleasing and calming. You can buy small bridges, temples, and pagodas in this style.

Left: Combining ornaments can be effective, but only if the shapes and colors do not clash. The natural snail shape complements the round and curving lines on the Buddha figure.

Above: A benevolent copper and verdigris faun guards the doorway of a house. This is a good way to grab attention, just as you do with pictures on a wall inside a building.

pots and planters

Every garden has some form of planter, be it a window box, little pots, or large built-in containers. There are many plastic ones available that have wonderful shapes and are easy to move around, even when full of dirt and plants. Give them a rusted look, paint them metallic, or cover them with bright colors.

Above: A stunningly elegant red against gray bricks turns out to be repainted, recycled cans filled with cacti.

Above right: Rust is a great look for pots, partly because the texture is similar to terra-cotta. Depending on the amount of solution you apply, the effect can be more or less orange or brown.

Right: Use pebbles in the garden to break up the planting and provide soft, natural colors.

Left: The beauty of this lovely arrangement is the wonderful mixture of texture, size, and height in the pots. The square, barrel-shaped, and tapered pots in old wood, rusting metal, zinc, terra-cotta, and paint stand out against a backdrop of black fence, white walls, and a blue door.

Above: These recycled oil cans have been painted in red and green. They are placed against a great wooden fence, on which are sprayed what at first seem to be decorative squiggles, but in fact are French words.

walls, fences, paths, and floors

The walls, fences, paths, and floors are the backdrop against which the garden works, and because of this, they are the biggest statement you will make in the garden. Paint the wall blue or yellow, and the whole garden changes. Due to the large area they take up, they are also the most affected by weather conditions—a wall or fence that glows in bright sunlight may be overwhelmed by a dark floor on a gray day—so they need careful planning.

Below: Pebbles can be laid to make patterns on the floor, like bricks. Most garden centers have terrific colors, sizes, and shapes that you can set in concrete, or just strew loosely as gravel.

Right: This beautiful, soft blue–colored house wall provides a great backdrop for the variety of greens in the foliage.

Above left: Bricks can be laid in a variety of different ways to make patterns, such as herringbone or the classic stepped pattern. Using bricks of different sizes and colors increases the possibilities.

Left: The beautiful colors of wood used for decking and pathways can be enhanced by wood stains or tinted varnishes, as shown here, or you can just let the natural color shine through.

Above: Disguise, or make your fence entertaining, by painting scenes on it. Here, little rows of houses are painted on the horizontal slats of a wooden fence, looking like terraces on a hill.

Left: Great slabs of wood, like stepping stones, make a raised pathway to the house, while large pebbles strewn on one side and grass on the other vary the texture of the ground.

Top: The soft shades of a lime-washed wall are a classic way of adding color to a garden of any size.

Above: Plexiglas sheets add color, texture, transparency, and reflection to a scene.

Left: Walls painted in shades of lilac add depth to a raised patio, beautifully setting off the natural, earth colors of the pots and wicker chair.

sheds, tree houses, and huts

Right: A painted trompe l'oeil silhouette is a simple way to create an illusion of space. With a cerise roof, white edging, and mauve painted wood, the effect is elegant.

The shed is the traditional retreat from the world for the man of the family, and even if your shed is not used in this way, it still has a sense of refuge. Most likely it holds garden tools, bicycles, and various pieces of junk, and is not at all romantic—but that old shed in your garden can still be made to look interesting.

Left: This delightful, romantic building is not quite a guest house, or a tree house. You can re-create a building like this by distressing old timbers, giving them a light wash or stain.

Above: Japanese gardens are inspirational, offering both tradition and modernity through uncluttered spatial design. The geometric exactness of this little black and white hut is simple and pure, making it the focus of attention in the garden.

Right: A new garden shed can be aged instantly so that it does not stand out like a sore thumb.

transformations

Color makes an enormous impact in the garden. If you want to create an immediate transformation in your garden, then start with a treatment on the walls or fences. The more timid among us should begin with smaller objects, such as a planter or a small side table, and experiment using the many techniques shown in this section. Using the clear step-by-step instructions in the projects that follow, you will realize just how incredible the paint-effect transformations are. The Aging Techniques (see pages 78–93) reveal a variety of classic finishes, including how to turn a used plastic pot into an antique-style rusted planter. Paint Effects with Color (see pages 94–121) includes an oil-staining technique, used on the "tablecloth" tabletop (see page 94), as well as stamped and painted houses (see page 118) that add decoration to a fence. Mosaic techniques range from a simple shell tablet (see page134) to a full mosaic floor (see page 122). As you progress, remember that many of the techniques shown here can be used on a variety of objects or features.

the projects

I have chosen 25 projects that represent a wide range of techniques for the garden. They are ones I have done for myself and for others, or ones I feel must be included in this book. I have used a wide range of paints and have tried to do projects that are not too difficult for people with little or no painting background. For those who do have a little knowledge about painting, these ideas and techniques can be developed. The little stamped houses project, for instance (see page 118), will look very different depending on who does it. This could be a great idea for a family project, with young and old working together, or for an accomplished artist. My little mosaic stool using old plates (see page 130) is also one that could be tackled by all ages. There are easy projects for beginners, such as the copper canvas chair (see page 114), the sand-painted striped steps (see page 120), and the painted decking (see page 106). The mosaic sphere (see page 136) is great for an accomplished artist.

I have tried to use simple, not too costly materials, most of which will be found in good hardware stores and garden centers. The variety today is much greater than it was several years ago, as more and more people realize you don't have to be a genius to produce some great decorative projects. My most expensive item was the Renaissance-style head made out of cement from a garden center (see page 86), which cost $80, but he looks about three times more expensive than the price I paid for him. Some of the projects, such as the green tree house (see page 116), the lime-washed wall (see page 98), and the garden shed (see page 90) are based on using interesting materials that might require a little searching around—depending on where you live, pigments can be easy or hard to locate, but these days with the Internet everything is possible.

An idea or technique that has been used in one project can be transferred to another item made of similar material. The painted decking is an idea that could be done on wooden fences or benches, for instance, and the painted houses could also be done on a birds' house or a table. Keep an open mind for possibilities as you tackle the projects, and your garden will benefit.

rusted iron pot

MATERIALS

plastic planter

750ml exterior iron paint

450ml exterior rusting coating

two 50mm paintbrushes

container for paint

container for coating

Easy to create and suitable for all your garden needs, this elegant planter is made from simple and inexpensive materials. You can use an old plastic pot, or simply buy the cheapest vinyl container available from your local garden supply center. It is quick to paint and finish, and the iron and rusting coatings also ensure that the planter is waterproof and weatherproof, so the finished project can decorate your garden throughout the year.

1 You do not need to prime the planter, but make sure it is clean and dry. Apply one layer of iron paint to the outside of the planter, then paint a 50mm thick border inside the rim. Allow to dry thoroughly for at least two hours.

2 Apply the second layer of iron paint, covering the pot and rim thoroughly. Allow to dry for an hour. While the paint is still damp, use a clean paintbrush to apply the rusting coating. Drag the solution roughly over the planter, using quick, sweeping strokes. Allow to dry overnight.

part-rusted chair

There is something very evocative about an old, white-painted ironwork chair delicately rusting in a garden—it brings to mind happy summers, perhaps sitting under a tree or relaxing in the sun. But such an old chair can be difficult to find, expensive, and not always in great condition. So it's better to find a new chair in the style of an old one and paint it.

The chair here is made of a light, gray alloy, and I painted it in an ecru color called Bleached Canvas, rather than a pure white, to make sure the result was not too new-looking. The rusting is not a paint effect but real rust, achieved by using a paint made from iron, which in effect is like painting with liquid iron. A rusting solution is then applied over the iron, and the result, after about 30 minutes, is real rust.

1 Paint the whole chair with water-based, off-white outdoor paint, and allow to dry thoroughly.

2 Dab the iron paint over the painted chair in corners, seams, and areas that might chip on a real iron chair—the feet, arms, and back are prime parts. For a realistic effect, vary the size of the iron from small spots to larger chips.

MATERIALS

alloy garden chair

750ml water-based, off-white, exterior paint

750ml exterior iron paint

450ml exterior rusting solution

1l sealer

two 50mm paintbrushes

two containers for paint

saucer for solution

container for sealer

3 Dab and dribble the rusting solution over the iron spots—it quickly becomes orange, and can be allowed to run into corners and crevices of the chair. When you are happy with the result, finish with a proprietary sealer.

faun's head

MATERIALS

plastic, cement, or reconstituted ornamental faun's head

60ml exterior copper paint

300ml exterior verdigris finish

two 50mm paintbrushes

clean cotton rag or kitchen cloth

container for paint

saucer for finish

Ideal as an ornament for a garden wall or corner of a patio, this bronzed faun's head, echoing the style of Renaissance Italy, is the result of an easy and effective transformation with metallic paint and verdigris finish. Aged and distressed, the faun adds a touch of humor that brightens up any garden spot.

1 Making sure the head is clean and dry, apply one coat of copper paint. Allow to dry thoroughly. Apply a second coat and leave until the head is damp but not wet.

2 While the second coat is still damp, paint the verdigris solution over the head in sweeping strokes. Allow the fluid to drip down the face for a few minutes. Soak the rag or cloth with verdigris solution and drag it loosely over the head. Then, using the rag, rub and wipe it over the face to stop streaks of the solution. Allow to dry overnight.

bird bath

Steel and aluminum are used widely in contemporary design and decoration. They tend to be expensive, so this modern, sculpturally shaped bird bath, made from gray plastic, gives you the chance to create the look at a fraction of the price—I painted it in steel, with a black tint in parts to give greater depth. Anything that is going to have water in it, such as a bird bath or a fountain, needs to be well sealed from water after it has been painted, using an exterior sealer.

MATERIALS

plastic bird bath

1.25l exterior steel paint

750ml exterior black tinting solution

2.5l exterior sealer

two 50mm paintbrushes

container for paint

saucer for solution

container for sealer

1 Coat the plastic with sealer and allow it to dry thoroughly. Paint the whole bird bath using the steel paint.

2 To give depth to the metallic look, paint parts of the bath with a black tint. Allow to dry thoroughly, then finish by painting the whole bird bath with sealer again, to protect it from water.

terra-cotta head

MATERIALS

reconstituted cement or stone ornamental head or bust

1.25l exterior terra-cotta paint

750ml exterior black tinting solution

two 50mm paintbrushes

clean cotton rag or kitchen cloth

container for paint

saucer for solution

Inspired by the golden age of sixteenth-century Venice, and a stunning centerpiece for gardens large or small, this wonderful heirloom piece is created from nothing more than a flea market concrete bust that is coated twice to look like an aged European antique. The accompanying plinth is transformed from white plastic in the same way, using the same materials.

creating the plinth

To create the terra-cotta plinth, choose an inexpensive plastic version from a garden supply center. Simply paint it with exterior terra-cotta paint, then follow steps 2 and 3 below. Allow to dry thoroughly before positioning it in your garden.

1 Ensure the head is clean and dry, then paint with two coats of terra-cotta paint. As you paint toward the bottom of the bust, make sure that you cover the rim of the base to avoid any of the original material showing through. Allow to dry overnight.

2 Paint the black tinting solution over the head and bust roughly, then wipe over with a cotton cloth soaked in the solution.

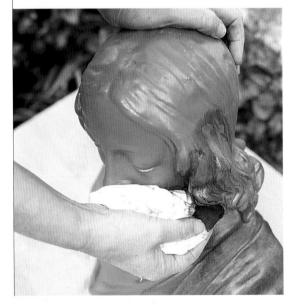

3 Using the cloth, rub over the bust as the tint dries, wiping and rubbing to prevent any drips and create an even finish. Allow to dry overnight.

gilded cherub

MATERIALS

cement or resin statue

600ml dark bronze paint

600ml gold paint

two 25mm paintbrushes

two containers for paint

Classical cherub or nymph statuary is well-established as a feature in the garden. When they were the prerogative of very grand houses, statues were brought from Europe, or specially commissioned. For most of us, there are now many very good classical-style statues available, made from cement or resin materials, at reasonable prices. In seventeenth- and eighteenth-century Italy in particular, the statues were sometimes gilded in part to give added emphasis and drama, so a swathe of drapery, or an item the figure was carrying would be picked out—the main statue could be made of bronze, marble, or even wood.

1 First, decide which parts of the statue are to be gilded to make them stand out from the rest. Then paint the nongilded sections with the dark bronze paint, making sure that you work the brush into all the folds and creases on the statue. Don't worry if a little paint gets onto the blank areas. Allow to dry thoroughly.

2 Apply the gold paint where you want it to be gilded—here, to the drapery and the plate—working carefully to ensure you don't go over onto the bronze paint. Again, push the brush into any folds so that the entire surface is covered. Allow the statue to dry.

garden shed

MATERIALS

garden shed

6l pale yellow water-based paint

4l crackle glaze

6l near-black water-based paint

6l exterior water-based varnish

three large paintbrushes

containers for paint

container for glaze

container for varnish

Black is a great background color for all plants and flowers, making a strong and definite statement. This shed stands in a bottom corner of a rambling, much-loved garden, so the decoration needed to have the right quality to reflect the garden. It required something that would reflect being well used and yet cared for, so I chose the look of old paint that had peeled and chipped off a little, showing the color underneath. The final, "character-building" effect was pleasing, and looked as though it had been there for years.

Painting the shed involved four layers, but in fact only the first layer was difficult to do, because the wood was dry and absorbed a lot of paint. To make the cracked-paint look you need to use a water-based paint—I used a creamy yellow color underneath to create the strongest contrast with the black finishing coat.

3 Paint on the second coat of paint, this time near black. Apply the paint a little more carefully on the areas where the cracking medium is, to avoid mixing in the medium with the paint. Allow the paint to dry thoroughly.

4 The final layer is a varnish to protect the cracked paint. Use two coats of strong, water-based exterior varnish, following the manufacturer's instructions.

1 Cover the shed with a layer of pale yellow water-based paint, working the paint into dry wood well, and re-covering areas where the paint has sunk into the surface. Allow to dry completely.

2 When the first coat is dry, brush on some areas unevenly sized patches of crackle glaze (peeling paint medium). Take care not to make these areas too similar in size by looking at the gaps in between the areas where the glaze is applied. Allow this to dry thoroughly—about 20 minutes.

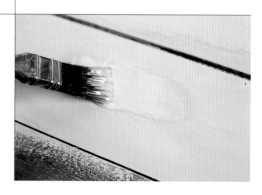

stonework pot

Visit a château in France or an old English country house and you will find stonework plant pots. Their weight, however, is immense, and the cost today is prohibitive. To imitate this look, I used a plastic pot with a rough texture, rather than a smooth surface, and turned it into a stone container. The pot has a chunky feel, and though simple in shape, the texture helps to give it the stone look.

A textured surface is not absolutely necessary, but the shape of the pot must be chosen carefully—it should be either classic and traditional, or very modern and minimal. Apart from plant containers, stonework can be painted on statues, spheres, tabletops, and garden benches. The colors of stone vary from soft gray-brown to creamy yellow, depending on the location and the degree of aging.

MATERIALS

plastic pot

450ml primer

450ml light gray exterior paint

450ml yellow ocher exterior paint

two 50mm paintbrushes

50mm bristle brush

container for primer

two containers for paint

1 Prime the surface of the pot and allow to dry completely. Using a soft paintbrush, paint the pot a light gray stone color. While it is still drying, move on to the next step.

2 With the base color partly wet, gently dab the pot using a large bristle brush with a little yellow ocher paint—don't submerge the bristles in the paint, just the very ends, so you can create a stippled, mottled effect. The main color should be the gray, so only dab in parts in a random way. The resulting color will be varied, as the yellow ocher will mix to a greater or lesser extent with the base, depending on the wetness of the first coat.

painted "tablecloth" tabletop

MATERIALS

wooden table

1.25l primer

1.25l white or off-white paint

1.25l blue paint

50mm paintbrush

25mm paintbrush

no. 6 paintbrush

straightedge

clean rag

container for primer

two containers for paint

A find from a lumber yard sale gave me a tabletop that was less than perfect for indoor use but great for a garden. I painted the one side with the best wood grain with a light wash of color, but painted the other side in a simple manner. This is a cheat's way of having a fresh, checkered tablecloth for an impromptu garden lunch. Copy my idea, or adapt it according to the shape of your table and its top.

Many people are fine when they just have to paint a flat coat of paint, but get nervous when they see any suggestion of brush control. Painting a freehand line is ideal, because using painter's tape gives a very hard line—a little wobble in the line is necessary to make the finished effect look like cloth, and there is always the danger of paint leaking under the tape. If you feel nervous about this, use a straightedge as a guideline—this could be the edge of a piece of paper—and don't be in a hurry to do it. As soon as you feel that you are going off course, stop and reassess. I decided to paint lines around the edge of the table—by the time the table was set, not a lot would be seen.

1 Remove any dirt and smooth the surface if necessary, then apply primer to the table and let it dry. Using the large paintbrush, paint the table with two coats of white or off-white paint, and again let it dry.

2 Lay a straightedge—here, I used a straight stick—to guide your hand to make the first blue line. Use the 25mm paintbrush, keeping the line as straight as you can, but not aiming for mechanical straightness. Alternatively, you can make two thin edges and fill in between them, but this is less satisfactory.

3 Allow each line to dry before putting the straightedge over it for the next one—a thick line and a thinner one alongside it makes a good balance. Use the tip of the 25mm brush to make the line.

4 Switch to a smaller, no. 6 paintbrush to make the thinnest lines, and to brush the thicker lines out if required. You could go on like this as long as you like, in theory, but the more you add, the more danger there is of either messing up or cluttering up the design—so step back and stop sooner rather than later.

staining wood

Staining is an alternative way to treat wood, both decoratively and practically. Decoratively it allows you to see the wood grain through the stain and add some color, and, at the same time, staining protects the wood by sealing it.

There are many proprietary staining products on the market these days, but the simplest way to achieve a stained look is to use standard latex paint thinned down with water. This gives a translucent, rather than a transparent, look, where the wood grain is apparent but partly obliterated, and is particularly good for a bleached wood look. You can also use lilacs, pale greens, or pale blues to give a hint of color. True wood stains are completely transparent and are available in a variety of colors from hardware stores, from natural wood tints to a range of greens, blues, and so on.

Pine is the most commonly used wood for staining due to its natural paleness, but it deepens in color over time, becoming more yellow-orange. To counteract this, a white, or even a slightly purple-blue color can be used to stain the wood, thus keeping the original pale theme.

1 As with stain, diluted white latex paint can be brushed on with a soft paintbrush. Make sure you work the stain into the wood grain, but be careful not to flood the surface with the paint.

2 An alternative method of applying stain is to dip a clean rag into the diluted paint or stain and work it into the grain gently, using both circular and straight movements of the hand, finishing with the latter.

lime-washed wall

MATERIALS

2l lime-wash putty

paint pigment; follow manufacturer's instructions, as pigments vary by color in proportions required

50mm paintbrush or old household brush

hard household broom or brush

container for mixing paint

stick to mix paint

newspaper

Dating from centuries ago, lime wash is a very traditional, ecologically sound outdoor paint that has reemerged as a trend in recent years. It has a unique, matte finish, yet gives transparency and depth to the color you have chosen. The paint is also inexpensive, and just a single coat will cover a wall quickly and effectively. While lime wash has an intimidating reputation, it is simple and easy to paint with, and although the mixing can be done the old-fashioned way, I heartily recommend buying the paint as preprepared lime putty and pigment. To mix your color, stir the putty well so all the lumps are broken down, then add small amounts of pigment, stirring slowly, to reach your desired shade. Lime wash can be used only on a lime mortar wall that has never been painted, or on brick surfaces. If you wish to paint a cement wall, a similar effect can be created with chalk paint, which gives a smoother, more even finish.

1 Brush your wall down with a hard household broom to clear dust and dirt. If you are painting the wall over more than one day, mix only enough paint for one session; lime wash does not store well. Stir the lime putty very well to remove all lumps.

2 Add the pigment in small quantities, stirring thoroughly to remove lumps and to bring out the depth of the color. However, for a rustic, streaky effect, stop stirring once the mix is smooth, and leave odd drifts of color in the mix. Now test the finished color of your paint; apply a small amount of wet paint to an absorbent piece of paper, such as newspaper, and allow to dry. As paint always dries paler than it looks when wet, you may find you need to add more pigment at this stage. Repeat the color test until you are happy with the shade.

3 Load a large paintbrush with lime wash and paint the wall. For this brick wall, I used an old, cleaned, dustpan brush, which is perfect for pushing paint into the uneven nooks and crannies.

blonde-bronzed patio table

MATERIALS

plastic table

1l sealer

600ml exterior blonde bronze paint

300ml exterior patinating finish

two 50mm paintbrushes

clean rag

container for sealer

container for paint

saucer for patinating finish

container for varnish

Here's a great way to do something interesting with standard white plastic garden chairs and tables. Finding an old table in my garage, I decided to see if I could transform it into something that looked a little more exciting and glamorous. The plastic needed to be coated first with a sealer, so the paint would adhere, then I chose a blonde bronze, the color of some old outdoor sculptures. It is a dark gold with great depth that has a green or blue patination to it. It is a good idea to experiment with the patinating finish on the slightly damp bronze solution on the underside of the table to see the final outcome. Vary the dryness of the bronze, and the final patination can be anything from pale blue to bright blue.

1 If you feel that the shiny plastic will not provide a good painting surface, brush on one or two coats of sealer, according to the manufacturer's instructions, and allow to dry.

2 Paint the entire table with blonde-bronze paint, aiming for a smooth, flat surface. Allow to dry a little

3 When the paint looks dry to the eye, but is not completely dry, splash on the patinating finish in spots, or lightly puddle it. Alternatively, drop spots of the finish in puddles and build up carefully with a rag, or let it run into any grooves on the tabletop. The bluish effect begins to happen within a few minutes, but wait about 20 minutes, until the solution has finished reacting. Adjust by adding more finish. When completely dry, finish by brushing on more sealer to protect the bronzed look.

blue-bronzed patio table

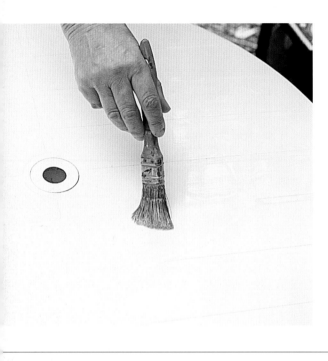

This is a variation on the blonde finish on the previous pages, using a similar technique and materials. Bronze has long been used to cast a wide variety of objects for both interior and exterior decorations. The color varies, depending on the mixture of metals, from a rich copper shade to a near black, and this in turn affects the color it turns as it ages. The blacker bronze ages with a white-blue effect, and was used on this glaring white plastic garden table, which has been turned into stylish bronze.

1 Apply primer to the table with a paintbrush and allow to dry thoroughly, following the manufacturer's instructions.

2 With a soft paintbrush apply the dark bronze paint, taking as much care as possible to avoid brushmarks—apply two thin layers rather than one, and brush out or feather with the tip of the brush to make the paint as thin as possible. Continue to the next step while the surface is still damp.

MATERIALS

plastic garden table

1l primer

600ml exterior bronze paint

300ml exterior patinating finish

1l exterior varnish

two 50mm paintbrushes

25mm bristle brush

container for primer

container for paint

saucer for finish

container for varnish

3 Dip a small bristle brush into blue patinating finish, and allow the solution to drip onto the still-damp tabletop. The more generous you are with the fluid, the brighter the blue and more obvious the effect. Allow to dry thoroughly.

4 Finish the table with clear varnish to seal in and protect the effect.

marbled pot

I needed a large pot that I could take in and out of the greenhouse, so it had to be quite light. One of the beauties of plastic is that it is so lightweight, and of the numerous plastic pots on the market, many have textured surfaces. This one was originally dark gray, with a rough, slightly graveled surface, not unlike the texture of a rough wall—by painting a mottled effect, it looks as if it has been cut out of stone. I chose yellow ocher and a gray with a touch of white to match the stones of the area I live in, but any stone colors could be used— the essential thing is to choose only two colors, and then by mixing them together you have a third color. Don't worry if they mingle too much—it's better that way than having them too strictly delineated.

MATERIALS

plastic pot

600ml gray-white paint

600ml yellow ocher paint

50mm paintbrush

two containers for paint

1 In separate containers mix two colors that are different but quite close in tone, such as a yellow ocher and a dirty gray-white. Stipple one color onto the pot, painting long and narrow areas as well as spotted patches.

2 While the first layer is still wet, apply the second color, making certain that you allow the colors to blend in along the edges. Don't end up with a severely defined line—the colors should blend together imperceptibly. Allow to dry.

painted decking

MATERIALS

decking

pale blue exterior paint

white exterior paint

water for diluting

50–75mm paintbrush or medium sponge

old brush for mixing

container for paint

roller and roller tray (optional)

Using wooden flooring in the garden for decking can transform a dull backyard, or can be used to make the transition from house to garden more comfortable. The problem comes when the wood itself begins to look tired and dull, as it fades and loses its freshness by being exposed to sun and rain—let alone snow and sleet.

My decking wood was not of the highest quality, so the surface did not have a really good grain that could simply be stained to make it look stunning. Instead, I decided to enhance the already gray look it had and give it a bleached look, but with a little blue. As an alternative to using a translucent and even stain, I used thinned-down exterior latex paint in two colors. The result is a light color applied slightly in patches, so that in some places the blue is more apparent than in others, and a little of the wood is discernible.

1 Mix the two paint colors together with a little water. Using a large paintbrush or sponge, wash the mixture over the decking. Try to work systematically and finish a square of decking at a time, because this stops two layers of watery paint from being applied on top of each other, which can result in a too-dense area of paint.

2 If your decking has gaps between the wooden boards, you can use a roller and tray for speed of coverage. Again, however, work with a system, and try not to over-cover any area, allowing the grain of the wood to be part of the final effect.

painted sundial

A sundial is a traditional favorite in many gardens. This sunflower was painted onto a southeast-facing wall, and there is as much decoration as there is information to actually tell the time. But it is a challenge to see how accurate you can make it.

For fun, we used a paintbrush for the stick that casts the shadow. You can add hour marks once the pointer is in place—on a sunny day, use a pencil to mark where the shadow falls on the pale blue area at each hour, then paint the hour marks in your own style.

MATERIALS

cement wall

150ml brown paint

150ml pale yellow ocher paint

300ml mid yellow ocher paint

300ml dark yellow ocher paint

600ml pale blue paint

no. 6 paintbrush

12mm paintbrush

hand drill or electric drill and bit

old paintbrush

five containers for paint

3B pencil

cement or mortar

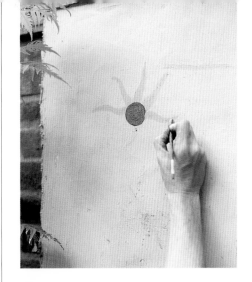

1 Decide where the design can go, bearing in mind that the aspect must be in direct sunlight for most of the day. Paint the central circle in brown, then start to add the lightest petals in a pale yellow ocher, using the no. 6 paintbrush. You can work freehand, as here, or if you are not confident with your painting ability, sketch the design faintly in pencil before you begin.

2 Switch between the various shades of yellow ocher to paint in the other petals, working on one shade at a time, and allowing each shade to dry. Use the brown of the center to outline the petals once they are completely dry.

3 Lightly outline the area for the pale blue, then use a larger paintbrush to fill it in. Use the smaller brush to paint the areas between the petals. Again, allow to dry.

4 Match the end of the "pointer" paintbrush to a drill bit, then hand drill or use a power drill to make a hole directly below the central part of the flower. Clean out the hole and stick the paintbrush in place with a little cement or mortar and paint over this when dry.

red and gold buddha

An Eastern theme is an appealing idea for a garden, and a single Buddha sitting serenely makes an interesting focal point. All kinds of Oriental-style statues and architectural pieces can be found in garden centers. Often made of cement or resin, plastic Buddhas may seem rather kitsch, but they look good painted.

I painted this Buddha red with gold over it so the red peeks out—in the East both are auspicious colors that denote wealth and abundance. The red jumps out at you in contrast to the green foliage and the matte of the leaves, distinguishing it from the shine of the gold for a dramatic effect. I painted gold over the red and distressed this to produce a little verdigris. This final step could be eliminated, because in some parts of Asia, real gold leaf is laid on statues as a part of praying. Real gold does not tarnish, but, to soften the harshness of the colors, I decided to tarnish it slightly.

MATERIALS

cement Buddha statue

300ml red paint

300ml gold paint

450ml patinating finish

two 50mm paintbrushes

clean rag

two containers for paint

container for patinating finish

3 The next part is optional, because gold leaf does not tarnish, but it does give a delicate and subtle look to the statue. Apply patinating finish with a brush lightly to the raised areas.

1 Paint the Buddha with red paint and allow it to dry. The red used in Eastern art is often a deep, strong red, but not as rich as crimson.

2 Take a gold paint and, using only the edge of the brush, lightly apply the paint to the raised parts of the statue. You can cover as much or as little as you want to. Allow to dry.

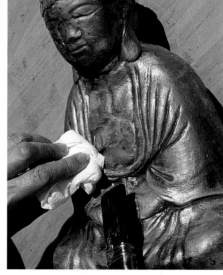

4 Before it dries, wipe off the excess patinating finish—too much can give the statue a heavy look and can distract attention away from the red and gold.

aluminum-style chairs and table

MATERIALS

wood and metal chair

wooden table

coarse-grade abrasive paper

1.25l rust inhibitor

2l exterior silver paint

white spirit

two 50mm paintbrushes

container for rust inhibitor

container for paint

duster

clean rag

These old, green-painted chairs are made of wood and metal, but the paint was peeling and the metal was beginning to rust, so the "shabby chic" was looking just plain shabby, and it was time for an overhaul. The silver paint looks like aluminum, a popular material in contemporary interiors. There are other silvery looks such as silver blues that can also be used. The new wooden table was a good, simple design, but the finish and materials gave it a workaday look. No special treatment was needed before painting, except making sure it was clean.

1 To remove the peeling paint and even the surface, sand the chair with coarse-grade abrasive paper, and dust off.

2 Any areas of rust on the metal parts must be treated. Paint rust inhibitor over all signs of rust, however faint, following the manufacturer's instructions, and allow to dry.

3 Apply two coats of silver paint, allowing the paint to dry thoroughly between the coats.

4 Degrease the table with white spirit, and paint it with two coats of silver paint to ensure a perfect, flat finish, again allowing the first coat to dry before applying the second one.

copper canvas chair

Old canvas chairs can look rather worn out as the sun fades them and they get dirty. I gave this old chair a face-lift using metallic copper painted directly onto the canvas. The metallic look in the garden is a very contemporary idea—the colors provide a neutral yet interesting backdrop to the greens and colors of foliage and flowers. Using metallic paint adds a new dimension—as it catches the sun it looks bright, and in the shade it takes on gray or silver tones, or shades of brown if painted gold or copper.

Choose a paint that can be applied to all surfaces—metal, wood, and canvas all need to be approached in a different way, but the same paint can be used. Other canvas- or fabric-painting possibilities in the garden include garden umbrellas and awnings.

MATERIALS

canvas chair

white spirit

1.25l sealer

1.25l metallic copper paint

two 50mm paintbrushes

clean rag

container for sealer

container for paint

1 Clean and degrease the wood using white spirit and a rag. Seal the seat canvas on one side only with a sealer and allow it to dry—on areas where both sides of the canvas will be seen, such as the back of the chair, seal both sides.

2 Paint the canvas with the copper paint—depending on the thickness of the fabric, you may need more than one layer to achieve a consistent effect. Allow to dry between coats and after painting, then seal to prevent dulling and tarnishing, and for extra protection if the chair is to be left outside.

green tree house

This old tree house was not getting much use now that the children are older, but the owners were reluctant to get rid of it altogether. I made a paint/stain mixture from linseed oil and green and white pigments. Linseed oil is inexpensive and has the property of very dried-out, old wood. The mixture can be painted on so the wood grain shows through like stain, or a thicker, more paintlike application can be made by adding more pigment—white pigment makes paint more opaque—alternatively, a second coat can be applied. This paint takes a longer time to dry than water-based paints, but is better than standard oil-based paints because of the high linseed content, which seeps into the wood.

1 Pour approximately half the green pigment (50g) into a container, then add the boiled linseed oil (raw linseed oil takes longer to dry). Stir continually with an old paintbrush to mix the pigment and oil until you have a fluid liquid paint.

4 When happy with the mixture, paint the color on the tree house. With old wood, the absorbency will differ, and you may need to paint twice over areas that are very dark, or those that absorb the most color.

2 Test the color by painting it onto a spare piece of old wood, as close to the color of the tree house as possible. If it is too dark, add white pigment a little at a time, stirring continually to blend the mixture.

3 Test the mixed colors until you come up with the right shade and opacity.

MATERIALS

tree house

1.25l boiled linseed oil

100g bright green pigment

100g white pigment

old paintbrush for mixing

50mm paintbrush

container for oil and pigments

painted and stamped fence

This is a charming way of bringing some color and an amusing design into your garden. It is very effective, and is a suitable project for a beginner. Stamping is relatively quick to do, and does not require any special equipment.

Next to the back door of my friend's house is a prominent but rather dull brown slatted fence that was in need of some cheering up. I began to think of ways we could make the area look a little more lively. I had seen some small simple houses painted on driftwood, so I decided to paint the slats of the fence in a similar way, repeating the pattern to create "streets" of cottages across the fence. The idea of this project is to create a simple look, rather than paint a masterpiece, so don't worry if you are not a confident artist. I used sponges to print the shapes because stamping is easier than painting freehand, and keeps the desired simple style. I chose ocher, a green-gray mix, a gray-lilac mix, umber, and a lighter green for this fence, but of course the number and choice of colors is entirely up to you.

1 Apply a color wash all over the wooden slats as a base for the design with the larger paintbrush or a sponge. You can choose any color you like—here, I used a greenish gray.

2 Once the shed is thoroughly dry, start the stamping process. Using a pair of sharp scissors, cut a foam sponge to make the house-shaped template. Cut a different template for each color you want to use to make the main part of the houses.

3 Load your small brush with paint for one of the house colors, and apply the brush lightly to your sponge. Press the sponge firmly onto the wood, and repeat with the next color on a fresh sponge. Continue like this until you finish a row, alternating colors.

MATERIALS

foam sponges (you will need one sponge piece for each color and shape you intend to use)

50mm paintbrush to apply wash

25mm paintbrush to apply paint to sponge

outdoor paint in a variety of colors

sharp scissors

container for colorwash

4 Load a small sponge with a darker-colored paint and run a line above the houses. Cutting smaller templates for windows, doors, and chimneys, stamp across the row, then repeat in a variety of colors.

multicolored striped steps

MATERIALS

one 600ml pot of exterior chalk-based paint for each color you choose

one 50mm paintbrush for every color you choose

50mm paintbrush for sealer

large bag of yellow or white coarse sand (285g of sand for every 600ml of paint)

clean cotton rag or kitchen cloth

wooden spoon or stick

two containers for paint

2.5l exterior sealer

wire brush

The steps leading out from my kitchen to the garden were looking drab, and I decided they needed some bright color to cheer them up. No single color seemed absolutely right, so my striped steps were born. As well as providing enduring color, this sand paint gives unity to varied garden surfaces; here, unpainted brick, smooth cement, and already painted areas are brought together. I used primary colors, but you could try a pastel scheme or a rainbow combination.

2 Stir well until the paint and sand are completely blended. Your mix should be a thick liquid that still allows you to use it as a paint. Load your brush lightly, then paint the first step from top to bottom in thick, sweeping strokes.

1 First, clean the steps with a wire brush and water to remove dirt and any weeds. Mix the first color paint with a handful of sand in a container, and stir. Keep adding sand and stirring well.

3 Allow to dry briefly to prevent drips, then repeat steps 1–2 for the remaining area. Once you have finished, allow to dry thoroughly overnight. Seal with a coat of exterior sealer.

pebble mosaic floor

MATERIALS

pebbles of different shapes and colors (minimum 50mm across)

slate pieces in two colors

large bag of gravel or aggregate

small bag of builder's sand

large bag of waterproof and frost-proof cement (you will need 4 parts cement to 1 part of sand)

trowel

rubber mallet

plank of wood

pointed stick and round planter

household broom

shovel

There is a long artistic tradition of using stones, pebbles, and even shells of different colors and sizes to create a sturdy, durable, yet elegant covering for a floor or even a wall. The tradition originated in Italy and has its roots in the stunning mosaic patterns of ancient Rome. I have always loved pebble mosaics because they produce such arresting color, pattern, and textural effects, and truly showcase the subtle natural shades of the pebbles.

You can either use pebbles you have found or buy them especially for the project. You can use stones that have been dug up in the garden, so the gardener's hindrance becomes a stylish resource. In a good garden center or home improvement store, you will see an inviting selection of natural products—you can choose from stones and pebbles of almost every imaginable color. For this floor project, I chose blue and green slates, as well as white and orange pebbles. As an alternative, you could try classic black with brown or lilac-tinged pebbles. When you are choosing your materials, it is a good idea to pick pebbles larger than 50mm across, because smaller pieces will not anchor as well in the cement. Try contrasting sizes and shapes for the different areas of the mosaic; the shapes can vary from rough, narrow slivers of slate or limestone to smooth, flat, and round pebbles.

Once you start making pebble mosaics, you will find it incredibly rewarding. Not only is this project fun, it will also make a dramatic difference to the look of your garden, and as long as you follow the instructions carefully, it isn't difficult to do.

1 Begin by marking out the area of the garden you have chosen for the pebble mosaic. If your garden has a rough cement floor (see left), you will not need to texture it. However, if you wish to lay the mosaic straight onto dirt, prepare the ground before you start. Fill the area with gravel or aggregate to a depth of about 50mm, tread it down thoroughly, then rake it level. This will give the cement a firm base and allow the mosaic pieces to fit evenly.

3 Using a trowel, make the cement as level as possible. For a larger area, you will find it easier to pass a piece of wood across the top to level the surface. If possible, find someone to help you and drag the wood across together.

2 Mix 4 parts sand and 1 part cement together. Then add water, continuously mixing until the mix is of a fairly stiff consistency. When it is ready, spread the cement over the area smoothly with a broom.

4 Next, mark out the shape of the mosaic design in the cement mix with a sharp stick.

5 Start putting the stones and slates into the cement mix. Begin at the center and work outward. Make sure that all of the slate pieces are lying in the same direction. Once you are happy with the design and pebble placement of a small area, start to bang them in gently with a mallet.

6 Mark out your central area of design; here, I used the perfect circle of a planter for size.

7 With the planter in place, keep working toward the center with the slate pieces and pebbles. As you complete a small area, remember that all the pebbles and slate pieces need to be level, so some will need to be tapped in more firmly than others; or simply tread stubborn pebbles in.

10 Once you have finished the mosaic, allow it to dry and set thoroughly. Do not walk on the area for several days.

8 Remove the planter and start to place the central area of pebbles. This is the focus of the mosaic, so be extra careful with the arrangement of the stones; be aware that the gaps between the stones are as visually important as the pebbles themselves.

9 Wet the mosaic slightly with a watering can, or sprinkle with a hose, for several minutes so the cement mix becomes wet enough to activate and set.

shell planter

MATERIALS

shells

planter

1.25l primer

1.25l black or off-white paint

white school glue

exterior varnish (optional)

two 50mm paintbrushes

glue brush for mixing

varnishing brush (optional)

container for primer

container for paint

container for varnish

I had been collecting shells for some time and had wondered how I might put them to use. The opportunity came when I had to make some planters for a dry shingle garden by the coast, where little grows except in pots.

Two wooden planters of different heights were available, but they needed decorating. I knew that the different heights would give a feeling of abundance when they were filled with plants, and that they could be set at different angles and added to. I made them stark and neutral by painting one black and the other off-white, and then decorated them with shells. If the planters were to remain outside in wintry weather, they would need to be varnished—and the entire side could be covered in shells.

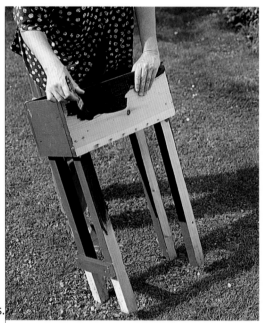

1 On a new planter, prime the whole surface according to the manufacturer's instructions and allow to dry. Paint the planter in two coats of your preferred color, allowing it to dry after each coat.

2 Apply enough glue to the side of the planter for each shell, and brush some glue onto the shells—the larger the area you can glue, the better the shell will stick. Hold the shell onto the planter until it adheres firmly, then move on to the next one. Allow to dry completely, and then gently brush on exterior varnish if you wish.

mosaic stool

Mosaic can be a very exacting business and needs preparation and thought. This method does not require great precision, because the smashed and clipped pieces of plate used are irregular shapes. Fitting different-shape pieces of tile together means that the gaps between the pieces will also vary, resulting in a random design. To get some sort of unity, collect pieces of similar colors or choose a strong grouting color to unify them.

An old, damaged wooden stool makes an ideal and interesting base for the mosaic as a flowerpot stand. But this style of mosaic can be used for a number of different things, from flowerpots to walls. The surface of this type of mosaic will not usually be very even, so it is not recommended for tabletops or chairs.

MATERIALS

stool

plates

1.25l primer

1.25l exterior paint

small hammer

tile clippers

white school glue

premixed colored tile grout

two 50mm paintbrushes

glue brush

palette knife

container for primer

container for paint

container for glue

clean rag

1 If you do not want to apply mosaic over the entire stool, prime and paint the stool, allowing it to dry thoroughly between the coats.

2 Use a small hammer to smash the plates so they break up into lots of pieces. Discard curved or raised pieces of plate, because these are difficult to stick down with glue.

5 When the tile pieces are firmly set, squeeze a little grout onto the surface, then spread it out evenly, using a palette knife.

3 Use tile clippers to "nibble" the edges of the large pieces of plate, rather than trying to cut right across the piece. You can decide the direction and angle of the cut very accurately by resting the clippers on the edge of the stool. Clip the pieces to roughly the same size.

4 Arrange the pieces, remembering that the gap between them is as important as the cut shapes. Spread glue liberally on the back of each piece. Apply a little pressure until it is firmly in place, then allow it to dry completely. Continue with the rest of the pieces until you are finished.

6 Allow the grout to dry a little, then wipe it off with a rag. If you do it too soon, the grout is lifted out of the gaps—too late, and it is hard to remove from the surface. Try a small area first before embarking on the whole mosaic. Allow to dry.

shell tablet

I saw shell tablets in a friend's garden and admired them. She told me that they are actually very simple and inexpensive to make. One small pack of cement mix makes approximately four or five tablets, depending on the size.

I was initially daunted by the thought of making a frame of wood to place the tablets in, but then decided to use old picture frames I found in a flea market. This may not always be the best choice, because the lip of the frame can get in the way when you try to remove the tablet, but you may find it preferable to making a wooden frame. Once made, the tablets are delightful for placing in the garden—in grass, or on a path, window ledge, or wall—and add a little splash of color.

MATERIALS

shells

picture frame

mixing board

waxed paper

6.4kg sand

6.4kg cement mix

3.8l water

bricklayer's trowel

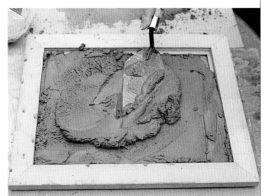

1 Cut the waxed paper slightly larger than the frame and place it beneath the frame—this will allow the tablet to be removed easily when dry. On the mixing board (an old, clean piece of plywood will do) mix the cement and sand mixture according to the manufacturer's instructions, adding water to get a smooth, working consistency when chopped with the trowel.

2 Transfer the cement mix into the frame with the trowel, making sure you put in enough to spread right into the inside edges, and smooth out any air bubbles. Fill to a little above the top of the frame. Wet the trowel and smooth the surface, removing excess cement as you go. Aim to achieve as level and clean a result as you can.

3 Gently press the shells into the wet cement, being careful not to press too hard and disturb the smooth surface. You can work freely and randomly, or you may want to sketch out the design beforehand. Allow to dry completely, then remove carefully from the frame and waxed paper backing.

mosaic sphere

MATERIALS

terra-cotta or cement sphere

felt-tip pen

pencil

white school glue

glue brush

tiles

tile clippers

cement adhesive

425g tiling grout

clean cotton rags or kitchen cloths

container for glue

container for grout

A sphere is a wonderful way of adding ornament to a garden. It acts as a kind of punctuation mark in a sentence. This mosaic was done on a terra-cotta sphere, but there are many other types available from garden supply centers that could be used, made of cement or other materials. This one has a flat bottom and a hole underneath, so in essence it is a large, round, overturned pot, making it both stable and light to move.

The sphere was decorated using subtle, natural colors that echo the earth, trees, and stone, rather than the bright colors of many modern mosaics. The background color is pale, with a straightforward and simple design of flowers, stems, and leaves. More bold and adventurous colors could be chosen to create dark or bright backgrounds and abstract designs.

adhesives

You will need cement adhesive produced specifically for outdoor work to withstand extreme temperatures. If the mosaic is to go on a wooden surface, rather than something very rigid like terra-cotta or cement, then a flexible cement adhesive needs to be used (see page 23 for materials and page 142 for suppliers), and tile clippers, gloves, and grout will also be necessary.

tiles

Tiles are usually purchased from craft stores, and come as square, oblong, or sometimes round units in packs. Use tile clippers to cut them to shape.

2 Seal the terra-cotta with glue to help the adhesion of the cement.

1 Draw the design onto the sphere in pencil and go over it with a felt-tip pen. This needs to be only a rough outline. Try not to make it too complicated, especially if this is your first attempt at creating a mosaic piece.

3 Choose the colors for your work by putting them out on a table and arranging them. A good general rule is not to choose more than three or four colors—a background color, and then, say, three colors to work together.

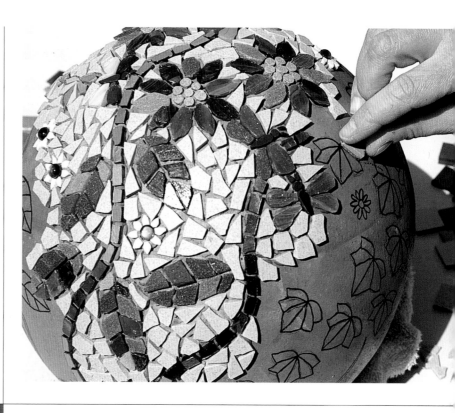

4 Copy the shape you want to make on the tile by drawing in pencil on the reverse side. Start with the shapes you are certain of, such as a leaf or flower, and then fill in the background with more random shapes.

6 Dab a small amount of the cement adhesive onto each tile and stick it on the sphere. There is no need to hold the tile in place as it dries, because it will stay unaided.

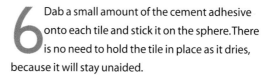

7 Finish each motif before moving on to the next area.

5 Use the tile clippers to nibble the tile into shape, rather than trying to cut large chunks at a time.

8 Mix the grout according to the instructions and then spread it over the sphere, rubbing well into the cracks. Wear rubber gloves at this point, because grout dries out skin.

9 When the grout begins to dry, wipe off the excess until it is all thoroughly cleaned off the surface.

10 Rinse the cloth used for wiping at regular intervals, otherwise the grout will smear over the tiles.

11 Switch to a clean, dry cloth, and continue to wipe and rub, thus preventing any drips and creating an even, smooth finish.

suppliers

Annie Sloan Practical Style
117 London Road
Headington UK OX3 9HZ
Tel: 01865 768666
e-mail:
paint@anniesloan.com

Annie Sloan paints and
products are online at:
www.anniesloan.com

UK

Bailey's Paint
Griffin Mill Estate,
London Road
New Stroud, Thrupp
Glos, GL5 2AZ
Tel: 01453 882237

Interior Affairs
Decorative Furniture,
Painting and Accessories.
6 The Grove
Westbourne
Emsworth
Hampshire PO10 8UJ
Tel: 01243 389972

Relics of Witney
35 Bridge Street
Witney, Oxon
OX8 6DA
Tel: 01993 704 611

Crick House Interiors
Weston Business Park
Weston on the Green
Oxon, OX6 8TJ
Tel: 01869 343007

The Stencil Shop
Eyam Hall Craft Centre
Eyam, Hope Valley
Derbys, S32 5QW
Tel: 01433 639001
email:lesley@
bcreative.fsnet.com.uk

Creative Decorating
Maranatha, Whitbrock
Wadebridge, Cornwall
PL27 7ED
Tel: 01208 814528

Webbs of Tenterden
51 High Street
Tenterden, Kent

TN30 6BH
Tel: 01580 762132

Spain

Annie Sloan España
Calle Gonzalo Barbero
No 12
18697 La Herradura
Granada
Tel: 0034 958 640632

Netherlands & Belgium

Linova
Laarstraat 74-76
7201 CG Zutphen
Netherlands
Tel: 0031 (0) 575 42300

De Vergulde Kwast
Westerkade 19
3511 HB Utrecht
Netherlands
Tel: 0031 (0) 303 40615

Duller and Co.
Van Oldenbarneveldstraat 82
1052 KG Amsterdam
Tel: 0031 (0) 2068 42332

Luxbros
NV Lerrekensstraat 32b
2220 Heist op den Berg
Belgium
Tel: 0032 (0) 15245555

acknowledgments

A thousand thanks to the people who let me do what I wanted in their wonderful gardens—Felicity Bryan, Mogs Crombie, and Bobby Stormont, as well as to Cathy Denne for all her energetic mosaics, such as the angel with a pot, the cracked plate wall, and the blue vase pot. A special big thanks to Jenny Quayle, who got out her shovel and joined in when we made the pebble mosaic in her garden.

Thank you also to all the staff at Yarnton Nurseries for being so helpful, and to everyone who helped out at my shop practical-style, while I got on with the book. (Yarnton Nurseries & Garden Centre, Yarnton, Oxfordshire OX5 1PA, UK; tel. (44) 1865 372124)

Many, many thanks also to Tino, Cindy, Georgina, and Ian for helping over a particularly difficult, wet summer—my still points in a turning world. Also thanks to David for holding the fort on so many occasions.

For the mosaic parts of the book I called on Becky Paton, who made the delicate mosaic spheres, the butterfly stepping stone, and the daisy pot. She can be contacted on becky.paton@ntlworld.com, and you can see more of her work at www.beckymosaics.co.uk

Many thanks also to David Kennedy, for the inventive sunflower sundial (tel. (44) 7816 594508), and to Limited Additions for the garden statuary. (Limited Additions, Park Road, Faringdon, Oxfordshire SN7 7BT, UK; www.limited-additions.com)

index